ANOTHER GHOST IN THE GALLERY
LOVE LETTERS TO THE BORDERLINES

JAMES KELSO

for starlight and the birb kween

Copyright © 2020 James Kelso

Cover: Monte McCleary

Cover photo: Samantha Pugsley, photographer, Shannon Grey model 2019

Author photo: Meagan Mishra 2018

https://www.instagram.com/samanthapugsleyphoto/

https://greyareaphotography.pixieset.com/

https://meaganhall.pixieset.com/

i hate to say you told me so or i said it
i have never felt your warm hand

i saw you leaving coming over the hill
from far away that's confusing i know

i never took you personally you know
i dont know that you ever took me at all

the relentless temptation of the knives
i know i have pulled on them too

i refuse to believe in doom
in inevitability we coulda we shoulda

its not that im not bleeding its just that
my heart is too full to empty here

all this burning down but I'm still here and
you're still here but you're not maybe were never

birdhouse or birdcage we differ on that
i never put on a door i swear i never did

i see the monster in your eyes
that cant be me so why is it me

am i a grave you've crawled out of
i only want whats best for you

this pile of dreams behind the abattoir
i cant kill them all i cant i cant i cant

all of this a well worn path
my slow footsteps so much

another ghost in the gallery
painted in our blood and hung
on the wall

what do you know of hell she said

see these fires these flames

i have lived here forever

these soft hands have rent my flesh

and fed me to the endless

it is a truth with her this prison

i can not will not dispute that

when she speaks i taste the burning

she fights to stay she longs to go

she will not burn me she says

she can not will not too close too close

what do i know of hell

i know a terrible secret

we know lucifer loved god yes ok

but what of god what of their love

cast away what you love forever

and you imprison us both

you think you saved me

you just built me my own cell

see these fires these flames

i will live here forever

either way the love is on the outside
and home is far away

its so funny that's been a thing
i even saved it for you this time
look look i bought a couch
we sat on the floor when was that
it seems so forever ago
before the splitting that dark lens
was anything real

i cant recall when it happened
it just always seemed to be there
i have loved you since the world began
i guess and i will even though that world is gone
there's no reason for it i cant break it down
into chunks of this this and this and maybe that
it just was and is and always will be
it is everything it is everything it is every thing.

such a bull in your china shop
i am sorry for that i guess but also not
somethings are better broken
so they can be swept away
but the cost oh void the cost
i didn't realize until it was too late
what the true leviathan lurking beneath was
you never wanted me to find anything just
look at the surface look at the surface
no waves don't make waves that attracts it

i watched it swim up faster faster
no teeth oh wait there they are
fascinating to watch it all unfold again
hello my old friend bring me the goodbye
i wonder if your memories are bathed
with that sepulchral light everything corrupted
every thing rotting and poisonous
the monster that makes me a monster

are we impossible now maybe
can you see it chained to you
its not you its just a parasite its not you i swear
do you love me enough to fight
i suppose not its hard not to feel the failure
but i will hold out hope i will hold out
and save you a seat on the couch

There's a Sephora bag on my
bathroom floor that's making me
cry these endings
which of us slipped the poison in
was poisoned
no matter the well, no matter anyways
you'll wander my corridors
i made sure of that
you see you burn as brightly
now as ever it will always be this
i will never go blind
you will never think of me again
yes good ok we move on

my immortal heart
you never understood that

the bag was i the
no matter
respect the distance the silence

i am thankful

look i am no surgeon no
cardiologist just a humble
combat medic stop
the bleeding kill
the pain get to
safety
i can walk and
smile and hello there
but make no mistake
i am severed and
the anesthesia is wearing off

in these rivers do you
(still) swim
threadbare and lofty
despite drought to spite

rock worn by petulant
persistent perspicacity
you always laughed
do you (still) laugh
in this home do you
(still)

love has that been forced
from your home a beggar
(still) a beggar
do they (still) hit you
in your sleep behind your eyes
when you stare at me do you
(still) see them or do you (still) see me
did you ever want me

to love you (still) did you ever
love me do you love me (still)
can I love you (still)
can we be (still)
are you (still)

in the far distance a bottle breaks
and sleep refuses my call.

I just had the sweetest dream
don't ruin it yet wait
if you fell I would

keep you so close
for always and
cover your face with

tiny kisses
and also with big ones
I would make sure

you always had toast
and napkins and
good water

and a hand
of mine
to hold

that is exactly
why you won't
fall but if you did it

would be because
you wanted
me

to do
exactly
all those things.

behold, chariot!
movement ways lit
secrets revealed and

paths led

the world bathes
in exultation
water and sky dance
in reflection
yet my day is forever

dark

without the light
of you

girl do you need to be held?
climb up here and let me hold you

are you a boy today?
climb up here and let me hold you

are you
everything and nothing?
climb up here and let me hold you

you are my
everything and nothing

will keep me from holding you
if you need to be held.

this dark ruler fear imperious
Narcissus power comes
not from the grave that beckons
but from hearts that do not

what you see in my eye
reflection of the wounding
you are not what you carry
i keep saying that

the crowns we bear
pithy metaphor for dominion
i am not come to you with chains
liberté! liberté! liberté!

am i not beauty enough to be true
i am indeed an ugly truth
you cannot look you cannot
its not the love thats blinding

you set my intentions assume me
in all things so monstrous
no love goes unpunished
how is this safety this is a bloodbath

if you cannot see me you cannot
love me you cannot know me
you cannot believe me you
cannot believe

how is it we are staring at
the same heart and seeing so
differently wake up wake up
i can see nothing but love

this is the tragedy you fight
so hard against every dream i hold
a surrender to love is a victory
against fear

a supplicant to death's door
i bring sacrifice
or maybe appeasement some
small offering to this time stay
your hand o please dont
take this away as well you have left me
with nothing

heart after heart i have
given away
come take one i have
one for you dear
for all that i have i have
given freely, greedily

i will grow another when you've gone
you can marvel at its intricacies
and feel nothing
for me am i

this worthless martyrdom
at the saddest of tombs

the god i cannot placate
oh void love is so small a word
yet too big too big not for me but
for the dead parade here have another i made it
just for you ok goodbye

what shall i do o death
if i stop laying everything at your feet
i will surely end
this feral mountain of flesh
is not death and is not enough

am i painting love for the colorblind
no i refuse i believe because i have been
and i have been taught to see
all the shades of you

here have another i made it just

this is by its nature a one sided conversation
you are not here to defend to explain
this is my storm i choose no harbor but
i can build the gallows the cross

i can decide
this is my kingdom
my memory of you is my prisoner here

i want to be kind

no cage you walk these halls with impunity
we talk i am sorry these are but snapshots
across so many lives so far away
remember that wait that wasn't you
but it was always me always me always me

i want you to know im not mad its not you its
this cruel life oh so many lives drowned i thought
well it doesn't matter now i cant blame you for
worlds so foolishly created

this is not punishment this is feeling its all
i can do if you want to understand this is mine
you didn't make me feel this i did i do i will

if i dont bleed here i will bleed everywhere
i hope you understand that
this is bread upon waters for those who need
this one sided conversation

as i let go of my wishes one by one
the one that will never fall
is for you to be

real

its an odd thing this black swath carved across my years
i haven't taken a breath in forever that didn't smell of gunpowder

hey i know who we love you and i its ok you know what I'm talking about
these love letters to the borderlines we love them we do we do we do

i wonder if they get delivered to pile up unread in well worn atria
do they keep them to reread on the darkest nights do they even know

how to read

they certainly don't write back

i have my own pile of return to sender no one lives at this address any more
thats what this is this elaborate hoax sending you what i cant send them

why do we do it because thats who we are and this is the hill upon which
we die again and again and fight for all in every time you do it too i love
that

no one has a calling card it starts like any other you cant know they don't
know
are we built to love the unlovable no one is unlovable you are lovable because i love you

i know love is transformative
because i have been transformed

i know love
in a world inside their heads what is real what is is it all black all black and
white what
you know that you are real i feel you are a triumph

to everyone in this entanglement let me tell you you deserve to love and be
loved
so much language "i am not broken" "i don't need to be saved" ok ok ok
but you need
we are accused of the darkest of intentions what can we prove to those who
cant see
we are the defiance of this most horrible lie no no no light for the blind

in echoes from far away you will come my last

you are loved you are loved you are loved

that damn bird you found that damn bird
i cannot forgive you for that
wait thats not right

you found that wee bird and i found you
i cannot forget that
thats it better

i have always seen all the way through
can you forgive me that
my turn to fear

i was so afraid was i right to be
no i wont believe that
i am not afraid

this is the future i saw in you
does it have to be that
is it this

have you done your worst
how do you do that
this fractal silence

do you sit in pause in memory
do you allow yourself that
do you feel me

it was only fear all just fear
can you believe that
nothing in the shadows

i am what i have shown i am
i can promise you that
these pages read them

our paths can rejoin ahead
if you can want that
light our dark roads

i have told you that
find us
wee bird

on this monument your hands carry or hold
it was such a whim she said pick it up
let me see wait add some of this
now a little i don't know i wasn't there
i just felt it and now that you're gone
you decorate my monument was it a poor choice
no its not like you've escaped from my everything
and anyways its a fitting scene for the death
of us of this dream

i cannot remove you from the story i wont remove
you from this i cannot remove i wont
remove you from the lightning in the pages
dammit how do i run out of words

how did you run out of me

i know i know it all makes sense you split and
it was all so much you took on what you believed
and you live now in your freedom and i respect that
but how

i struggle do the work to understand to dismantle
so much is not me but you ran from
they follow is that who you fear
my own road well worn
come despair come despair
your fight is not with me
but you have still won

do neither of us know what lies in your heart
what is real and what is poison from your hands
or mine those hands
that grace this
my pyramid my love seen from space
those hands i have never held i keep pointing that out
but hands i wont let go of

no that is the answer to all of this
we both fight me isn't that funny
you because you fear me
me because i love you
who wins if who wins

on this monument your hands carry or hold

i dont talk enough about the good days
the great days the 5 AMs and feesh
the remember whens that buckle me
as i watch the clock tick you farther away
grinding bone on bone you said no
you don't understand or maybe you just
dont trust this was amazing hard work yes
but worth it yes so much
i am drowned in all ways look not
by you but by this lack of my god
what do i do when i cannot breathe you
so what sometimes i cough

you are imprisoned not a prison

these guards are not you these bars are not you
i just wanted to hold your hand while
you plotted your escape
there was nothing to break us
ok writing all this is a lot i know but
you know I'm dramatic and this is just
a snapshot not the story

i got more ramen today i cant seem to give it up
i cant i cant i cant believe this story is done
jesus every word is a plea how did i come to this

i dont know if i ever saw the claws
i swear i tried to

am i
the wound or the weapon

i dont talk enough about the good days

you growled at me no i didn't it wasn't that
yes! no you said but that come on that
was funny we laughed a lot, it doesn't seem like it
these snacks are poison! i think i brought too much scotch
id bet folding money that dresser lies unmade

i told you i wasn't going anywhere you said it felt like i was
i was right there tho, right where i am
i always answered my masters voice i hear and i obey
so much glitter on such shiny people you always glow to me
you always glow to me can i see it

i hope you write that story - i hope you write all the stories
oh the moments you ran like quicksilver too few
you'd raise your fists in victory its not an argument tho
every moment was triumph i swear it
i never cared for winning only you

im a model you cant afford me you stared at me ha!
that space will never not hold you to me
how was that heaven it always was not now tho
wait which of us is the devil which of us is cast
this is supposed to be fond

i think you never really liked my music thats ok
you still said do it and miraculously i did
not what you expected but thats good isn't it
i dont know what you think of the book or
what you'll think of this one

i have a brain full of reasons of evidence
i am after all a man of the science of the navigation
even now i see you turn eyes like ancient glaciers
corners of your lips move imperceptibly upward
this i think i want this forever yes

i want a forever of too many books and loose
sweaters and whiskey and look what i made
yes of blood and fire and heavy lifting and
thieves in the castle and we do what we can
and whispers and bells in the darkest of darks

we still have suits to try on and snow lights and
horseshoe knives and prompts and lighthouses
and ostriches and dreams and dreams and dreams
you will dream them with others and move on like glaciers
and the only thing forever is the silence

let me tell you this
no matter what you take
you destroy what damage
you cannot sneak
back into my heart
and steal
my love for you
that is mine
and I will cherish it always
and if you ask nicely
I may take it out
and show it to you
again

i find myself
in late nights early morning
listening against the silence

i cant explain
so much color so soft
you made me

so soft i flowed
out from my fingers
an endless gentle feast

i was dead you see
you think you are
dead but you are soil

this is not the end
of what we have planted within
each other so carelessly

this is just
the winter yeah its cold
but spring is coming
i promise we have yet to bloom

it is my most fervent
wish that
death is the end
for as long as i am
i will feel
the loss of you
and that will turn
even an eternity
of heaven
into hell

whisper
your love you
scream
everything else
what they hear is
all the sharp
and the dark no
wonder they turn
away
your tempest scores
me no less i just believe
in your eyes so i stand
my ground
and listen
to find the calm
and hear
the whisper

Starlight,
have i painted you
to your liking no you
protest
is my
hand unkind my eye
it is not what you know what
you see a void
the coal of your wings heavy
and burning
empty
of light of life
no in you i see
all colors entwined
warmth of eye and light
of feather
when you gain flight
will you soar or flee

across this moat
we stare our
engines of war
our walls these
stones a silence
such dark water
we have both fed
our drowned
to the gap
but the battle
for this bridge
is not between enemies
i seek not dominion
or dominance
I cross this
to be close to
share a fire a hearth
a home
I come to these lands not
to be your conqueror
but to be
your champion

what more do you want
I cried
no she says I want
less
so there it is
and now everything
between us
is distance.

i cant see they said
how you can do
this i feel am i
dying yes
a bit of course
a part of you is
gone and it took your
dreams with it
youll feel better
if you can let it die let it die
count that as a blessing little
heart
but you dont? no
nothing i plant dies i tend
this garden always
then when does it stop
hurting
if you do it right
never

how long were you
building this tomb
was my name carved
on every stone as you laid
them
or is it built upon ruins
upon ruins upon
are these foundations
as old as you
are
i did not see the walls coming
up until i noticed the light
getting fainter no you said
nothing is changed
here
the last stone sealed me in
you out and covered in desert
lost to time you forget
what I cannot
wait
you have buried me as
deeply as you can you
are no archeologist i am
no quiet ghost I will forever be
the wails that shatter
on the face turned away

these are the times i miss
you the fallows of night
with bell and torch
id wait you know until i knew
you were sleeping my vigil
done for the night come morning
come as we speak such mornings
such mournings now
the skittering of such tiny truths
nestled in the horses of myth our
myths i always saw the truth that
scared you it shouldn't i am
no fortress
i no longer need keep watch
my masters voice silent
i am an empty belfry a
forgotten waypost
i will rest in the barrow of my
sentinel failure, buoyed by a moon
and the faint sound of laughter
an unnavigable distance away

A rumination on three paintings by Carolyn Hitt

I want to tell
you a story you see
that painting was a friend
and i
we faced the moon
not touching but close
I had maybe a selfish
selfish dream it got
painted too maybe
it was a maybe but now
it is just a painting
the third painting black
and torn torn torn
apart
is called patience it might
mean hope or not but
this is no imitation this
is love this
is life this
is art.

put me down slowly
Starlight, you always knew
barn door open into floods
did you even look up

i wonder do you hear some
ticking or a countdown
from the moment we met

is it a relief to know the end
is in your hands

no need for dreams you know
nothing to miss
you wave from inside the burning
and make me walk away

Starlight, your sky is empty
while mine of full of you

split me black swallow
it all the late night moon
won't shine unless you let it
each line cut from this
book this story this
flesh i can't i won't
i will die laughing
in these ashes
because you don't get
what do i know of
you don't get to make
me hate you
this door stays open for
ever and you can't close
it you might as well
walk through it.

this is it the bag over
my head shallow water forgiveless
such heavy shoes so much blood

you said you said
i know you didn't know but
i said i said

how the last feather falls seems
such a capricious dance
yet the trajectory - down - is
inexorable, predictable

a path leads to a frozen grave
beaten by footsteps long and away
cut through the perfectly flat glass
one speck of grit lies there

and all things end
at a mote i have moved a thousand times

she said she doesn't know what love is so what

does it mean when you tell me you love me

i smile nod yes interesting your theories

(i always die here oh well)

what do you hear when i say i love you

chains and then footsteps, I'm sure

its ok anything you need

dust in the air like a curse

an unechoed gift one

drop and then

hold fast, Starlight
I see you radiant
fire born of fire
you fear the night
buries you in silence
your patch of sky so small
those who see you
from so great a distance
would name you mere
and claim you in constellation
yet for the one who holds
the tightest orbit
a sun
hold fast, Starlight
I see you radiant
let fire be born of fire

you
devour me i
will feed you
slice after grinning slice
my blood laughing
down your throat
we both ache to feed
you
think starving is a virtue
little bites yes delicate
a sliver from here, there
no consume me let me
all the way in
let me soak into your bones
you
didn't ask for this
hunger i didn't ask for this
either this is admittedly
unsustainable but
we feed to grow
you
will devour me yes and i
will smile because i know
what you don't for i am
love and hope and love
and you are what you eat

meet me in the endless
dance magic across the teak
of old ships and the sorrow of the moon
catspaws and dandies is this
divine so divine

i want to hold your hand
so tightly we can swirl like stars
yellow wines and silverlight
is that yes i believe so
falling in

i dream of your well
everything wrapped around me
the catch before the kiss
moments like chandeliers light me
light o gods light

if there was magic i swear i would
rip this dream from the gods
but there is none
and sleep, my love,
has vanished

is it first snow
already i tried to keep
the path clean

it was not to be
overgrown and rendered
impassable not by
my hands anyway

i have built a silence
each screaming jackdaw and
crying jay soothed
or dispatched

i wait for the bonesnap
of your footfalls
i fear i fear
they will never come

so i keep the path
clean
and the way
silent

is it first snow already
maybe i should rest

it is a curious thing this knot
i cannot find start nor center
each coil a mystery or maybe
an answer

funny things, they are
do they restrain or keep
does this need to be
tightened or undone

it is a breathtaking fantasy, the sword
an easy cut and it all falls away
but a knot destroyed is not solved
i cannot love a ghost, not again

place my hand where it needs to be
i don't think you know yet
so let's go over everything
until we know o i would love that

i have one too you see
and i have wishes, o yes
eyes fingertips oh the small dark
we seem so close please

listen, love, listen
delicate, now, there, a cut careful
we tie, and find one another
again again again

free what must be freed
bind what must be bound
let loose the unkind threads
and weave between us everything

their feet moved
crossed under the tea
table shifting
"look," i said
their eyes remained fixed
on the cups unwavering
"you are not going to wake up
one day and be in love with me
you are going to wake up
one day and realize
you've been in love with me
the whole time."

if I'm just better
tame my unruly intentions yes
so many boxes so small can I
even be that small

o no child i will never
you be bigger you be
(why is this a fight)
bigger fill me yes drown me
fearless let us be fear
less

no one ever believes me but here
i am i have scoured the library
for what we have forgotten
its not that i have courage you lack

bury yourself in me let me water you feed you
more more YES more YES MORE
bury me in you and let us bloom
all the way to the top till we are in sun

roots in the dark, we grow till we shine

she says look
i have this
the chains shift slightly
granite follows her like plague
i am strong
yes i say i see the marks
blood on the chains and scars
on the ground i am humbled you know
but as it is your nature to love
that which you have dragged so far
rightfully proud of that distance
it is my nature to love
your wings and wonder
if you were free of these burdens
how far would you rise?

in the end it all comes
down to this, this
end

i face it and see
who blinks first
chicken
on this abandoned road

i am not a martyr
or masochist
i truly believe
every time i am just
if you just is this just

this scarless moment weightless
all wounds and wings
you were always worth it
in all ways worth it

im sorry
but you always let go

i never will.

here i draw the line here no more
this has done what
sorry i am made of knives you say
i want someone bulletproof
but they can't feel what

you need them to feel safety
is not safety it is control and
static reinforced

enabled.

you hurt me i heal you break
my heart i grow more you kill
me you want the soft prison ok
everything padded so you can't hurt
it'll kill you too you know that

this is my love letter to you borderline
cut me cut me drown
in my blood is love
not a cross but a choice

this hand outstretched
is forever
yours

I will drag the memory
of every heart I have
given away with me

until they are enough
to fill a grave
in which I long to rest.

such a distance it seems
did i imagine no wait
there it is we get
closer i see it
clearly

that light it makes
people run the heat
the fire its just
Starlight

alone i smile terrifying
you what do you
do with that cry
you'll burn like the rest

yes let the last
thing I see be your brilliance closer
than anyone

hold me i am fireproof
for I too am made of flame

for Rachel whom i loved

haunt me let me
feel your whisper

on my neck my
chest once

move the books move
me to tears

come haunt me your
ghost anything is

better than
this empty

space where
you belonged

and are not

does the grim ash of
polluted tombs
grow you pretty, one color
in the poison dark?

shallow, so easily unrooted
that which is beneath you
is beneath you this
fear of floods

grow, or don't. i will
bring what water i can no
matter where you are, how
ever far it must be carried.

here, casket rose,
a blossoming tree,
from my eye to yours
in better soil your dreams lie.

let them see you brave
bedrock feet and bend
the light around you yes

the wilds and winds live
in your eyes fearless for
a moment as many as you can

chase the dawn so greedily
devour the nights how magic what
magic oh you are so

scorch it your path you cannot
i will not down the
Starlight let it fucking burn

and when your courage fails
and the wailing no stop o god
are too much too much again

let me see you feel my hand
here, love, here, please
tremble

if you see a
rhythm to my step a
tap tap tap in
time
in sync with
the trees as
they reach for far light
blossoming
if you note the sway
waves under
the breath of
wind
in my hips
a clockwork joy
the mainspring of my
world
i carry you
every moment in
my heart like a
song
and I
cannot
help but
dance

you took my arm

"what of thorns"

trust is the soil
in which we bury love

"what of fear"

you grabbed my hand as we
crossed the street

"what of forgiveness"

shhhhh it is still young season
and everything

has time to grow

time has done
its work and ash
surrounds everything

i have come to find the silence comforting,
a reminder of fate and inevitability
this, this is where i belong

so much in threes
to think i was so full
of love so short a time ago

i will hear your voice again,
and you will win your control
a safe distance

calm, let us not risk
a sensible house we'll build
please, sit, pretend

but i know your unopened rooms
and your knots and your flames
and i will show you the meaning

of love, forever.

www.ingramcontent.com/pod-product-compliance
Lightning Source LLC
Chambersburg PA
CBHW031505040426
42444CB00007B/1211